Elegy for Desire

Camino del Sol

A Latina and Latino Literary Series

Luis Omar Salinas

elegy for desire

The University of Arizona Press   Tucson

The University of Arizona Press

∞ This book is printed on acid-free, archival-quality paper.
Manufactured in the United States of America

10 09 08 07 06 05   6 5 4 3 2 1

Library of Congress Cataloging-in-Publication Data
Salinas, Luis Omar.
Elegy for desire / Luis Omar Salinas.
p. cm. – (Camino del sol)
ISBN 0-8165-2462-9 (pbk. : alk. paper)
1. Love poetry, American. 2. Mexican Americans – Poetry.
3. Aging – Poetry. I. Title. II. Series.
PS3569.A45943E44 2006
811'.54–dc22

2004026291

Publication of this book is made possible in part by the
proceeds of a permanent endowment created with the
assistance of a Challenge Grant from the National Endow-
ment for the Humanities, a federal agency.

Contents

I   The Luxury of Darkness

II   Men at Sea

III   Chivalry

IV   Dreaming under Gray Clouds

V   Elegy for Desire

I the luxury of darkness

Intro

I love introductions, possibly because
They make you look smarter than you are.
And my personality, peculiar as it may seem,
Is generous, and one of the reasons I use a cane
Is to beat off mad dogs.

The most difficult poems to write
Are those of love and those of death.
I'm half in love and half dead.
It stands to reason that I've come upon a difficult task.
The dead can't complain, and lovers always do.
Well, I'm here, and that is important.
And if life can be as exciting as this,
I must be doing something right.

Here and Now

I am Omar, the Mexican–English–Byron,
Aging with disillusion and contempt
As I listen to the sermons of sad fools
And loony puritans – angry as I lift a poem
To their dog ears, and the autumn leaves
Fall like them on their leaf faces. . . .

I don't mean to offend, yet how can I not
Renounce heaven with man's evil–eyed
Indifference, and desire, instead,
In the here and now, love?

I would be free of the bigotry and
Low sham of politicos and the despotic
Travails of the ill. Let the River Lethe
Run its soothing unguents and
Water my thoughts with confidence,
A white shirt, good cologne, and the candor
Of a bright lady's smile, as I stop questioning
Venus and make friends with idleness
And the poetry of Ovid while the world
Changes around me. Let these torrents
Of late summer, my personality of autumn,
Know others and know myself.

Don Luis II

When I'm cruel, the world is mine –
when I'm gentle, animals hate me.
I feel like tossing fruit at politicians
and giving poems to beggars.
I'm Don Luis with the passion
and the language of a flamboyant
spendthrift. I don't know how far I can go –
no doubt I'll astonish the English
with couplets, perhaps travel to Italy
and learn to sing *bel canto*?
Whether my poetry thrives
on wisdom or on foolery, it's too early
to tell. I'm on my way to Greece
to pay homage to Sappho, to sing
on the isles and catch stars
while they dance in the heavens
like earrings on ladies' ears.

My Gentle Dog

I need a dog
That can stand
Up for me
When the nights
Get mean and cold;
One that can bite
A harassing stranger,
Instead of me
Using my wit.
If I outlive him,
I'll provide
The proper burial
And a headstone:
"Here lies Omar's dog,
who died, poisoned
by the world, who
guarded everything
but his heart, who
was so melancholy
he reminded me of me."

Ode to the Night Air

Away from the university,
Happily listening
To the tolling of bells,
I try to make sense
Of a box of oranges,
Moths playing cruel games
With the light bulbs,
The sagging patio
Showing its age,
And my face,
Which has forgotten
Itself and needs a shave.

I have a quiet passion,
But the math doesn't add up
And theories fail
To calm me.
Away from the hardheaded
Professors, I've prospered
On the same paths as before:
Life is a maze of
Amazements
Flashing a weak smile –
Success is a piece of a star
Drowning in the air,
And a man's fascination
With fame stumbles

Like a lost drunk
Through the barrio.

Loneliness has been
My neighbor all my life –
When I was a kid,
It used to follow me
Home from school;
Even though I was a favorite
With the nuns,
I could not pretend
I was abnormal.

The world has no use
For madmen – self–deception
Grabs at the throat;
Disillusionment is thick;
I feel like a rejected suitor
Who has misplaced
His bow tie,
And the night air carries
Its homeless message.
Who am I now?
A reactionary?
I've dreamed myself,
This rootless traveler
Who knows
Even the dogs are lonely. . . .

Pacific Wind Tossing Pebbles

How do I behave with a poet's
Heart – tossing pebbles
At the Pacific wind?
I am the aging mariner
Of his youthful loneliness,
Lacking prudence, sailor
In a sober sea. . . . She,
In her green bathing suit,
The surf around her breasts
As I embrace the moistness
Of the sea, a suitor with charm
And illusion, walking away
From the brooding sky, another
Hamlet dead in the water.
I rebound, individualist
Wounded ever so slightly
By life's torn ligaments
And beautiful women.
This sincerity congratulates
The sea for not having drowned us –
A smile, a wish, is all I own.

Sea Gypsies

The ocean tosses like a Chopin etude.
Her green bathing top flashes
with the sun's light like a dancing fish,
the surf around her waist – and I think
of a girl from my youth who married
young and died young. I miss her
as much as I miss the sea and
the early autumn seagulls that speak
with the silver tongues of rhetoricians.
I carry the image of her bronze body
with me, her Virgin scapular, her silver-
aqua eyes, along with a Greek hymn
that haunts the sea crags, that haunts
this beating surly mollusk of a heart
as I watch the gypsy fishermen
arrive in their ghetto boats
with princesses dressed in scarlet,
in deep blue with long black hair and
scarves, snakelike necklaces around
their pearl necks, breasts covered
by green silk and gold medallions.
It must be fun to be sad gypsies.
I tremble from their capricious kisses
and tumble on the cool beach, tossing
in the salt foam, crossed by passion
and the perilous waves that whistle
on the rock like a crazy woman.

My Melancholy

I don't know which cloud I'm on.
It would be nice to have you
Sitting here with me, with the music
Of butterflies in the air. These half–
Satyr legs tread toward where
The stars stared through your eyes,
Where I surrounded you like summer,
With the robins' fighting and my mood
Unpredictable.
             You are off
To the Bahamas, and I'm here on
The mainland rubbing noses
With the natives, examining the ocean,
The sand that grabs at your ankles
Like still–burning bits of fate. . . .
Gazing from the shore, the sun
Never seems to go down, and many miles
Will always be left for me to get to Greece.
May happiness follow you like a seagull
That dances on the wind. I'll sit here
And watch the pelicans drift by
Like snowy white clouds . . . missing
My early chums who have sadly gone
To rest, and though my heart is worldly,
I am nothing for the afternoon to ridicule.
As much as I confide in humanity
I'll take no more drinks with nature –
And leave the rest up to God.

Idealism

I cling to earth with all
my earthly aspirations
for the muse, the lust
of a lyric drowning in her
dark brown eyes as I kiss
the sweet pears of her breasts.
How could I be poor with such
beauty or have sadness stroll
me through the streets
like a loon?
           With bits of paranoia
I could devour the wind, but
who wants to walk alongside
illusions, illness, my instinctual
love? I am after fame, a romantic
fighting for a documented version
of his life, crazy without love,
and crazier with it.
           I admire
the Greeks – and my parents
for having raised me. Had the Greeks
raised me, I'd be in Italy right now.
My mother's in ill health, and
my father is dead. Most days
are like waiting for a pecan to fall,
and I live on dancing air.

The Sea That I Abandoned

As your love unbuttons the clouds
And I open my eyes
Like your flowered body,
Which has been drowsing like mine,
While September sings
In the bird trestle of your heart,
Your bosom with the melodious songs
Of a light wind, your aqua eyes
Like starlings in the yard,
I think of the sea that I abandoned
As a child.
                    Now older, seeing you,
I am reminded of the seagulls dancing
In the air like ballerinas above the beach,
God's lovely creatures in their miracle
Of flying eloquence, dressed in cloud–
White, speaking an aquatic language
All their own, a complaint beyond love.

The Night Opens Its Arms

I have but one life to give
to poetry and the ladies –
I will hand them a ripe
pear of bruised love.
What luminous eyes guide
them or me, guide darkness
and our mad faces as I stumble
into the quiet bitterness
of early spring?
                    And under
the clouds, your gray
eyes, your early apricot
kisses, picaresque and soft,
as we listen to the winds,
the entwined foliage
of our hearts, the petaled
emptiness of the moon
as it glows onion–white
where the night opens its arms.

The Luxury of Darkness

I live the life of a stargazer,
watching the leaves fall off the trees
as I doze off reading Agamemnon again.
I do have the luxury of darkness,
which clothes me like the Paris
of my house – dressed in green velvet,
I have nothing golden or otherwise
to offer to the stars. But the lucent
stars cheer me, and the eminence
of the brooding landscape I enjoy
before I lose my temper, and the nymphs,
intent on ruin, jump into a pool darker
than their hearts. A bit confused,
I try to make sense of my tragic kingdom
and the fierce clouds as I name
the hazy constellations, one by one.

II men at sea

Men at Sea

Let's go whaling, men – bring
your harpoons and plenty of salsa!

I'm sweaty. I've just had a bowl
of clam chowder, my friend
is going insane and can't hold on
to his spoon. My new book
has the price of a cheap dinner,
contending the end of my classical
period – now it is the romantic –
love, biography, and elegy.

My friend is going more insane
for the ill treatment he's gotten,
and he's turning on the oyster crackers –
pieces of bitterness are falling
from the clouds.
                    My audience is both
ribald and intelligent, and though
I walk using a cane, they are unmindful
of the most magnificent thing about life –
its recklessness that washes us all
out the door.

When I Was Young

When I was young I knew
The sea, running on cold, wet sands. . . .
I remember Christian swimmers,
Fishy airs, the sun, piers that touched
Far into turquoise water, and ladies
In white who threw light
Laughter from under their parasols,
Like kisses.
           My love for the sea
And the ladies, pieced together
From fragments, dreaming
When I was young . . .

No Don Juan

I'm no Don Juan –
I'm just a regular guy
When the ladies
Are there, impulsive
In a loneliness
That follows darkness
Home like a starving dog.
I live bittersweet
In the late spring rain.
An ocean breeze
Can sweep me away, like you.
I do not drown,
But drown in the arms
Of a woman. The surf
Takes me in, the rolling
Waves seduce me
Like ballerinas
With their feet on the foam.
Let me make love with a world
Of spring thoughts as I kiss
Your sweet ankles and ripe arms,
Softly touch your eyebrows
Before darkness falls on us.

Studying Abel

I left my cane in England,
My heart in France,
And my mind in a sanitarium
As effortlessly as I leave
The lady with a patent leather purse
On the street pestering me.

"Where's Omar?" they ask in Florence.
"He's in England, writing a poem
About Cain."

"And what was he doing in France?"
"He was with the ladies studying
Abel."

I love poetry so much, I hate
To give it up
For a little salvation.

Beethoven

Who hears the silence
Of the lovebirds who
Linger in the evening
Rain like passengers
Aboard a ship?

He can no longer
Listen to her dancing,
Walking, or singing Italian
Arias – the woman
With the hair
Of sunlight on
Autumn leaves. . . .

He yearns to caress
The raindrops
Between her breasts
As they lead to
Her music in an
Afternoon of rhapsodies.

Shelley Drowning

I see Shelley drowning.
I can't save him.
I can barely save myself.
And the worst of it is
The melancholy at the
Campsite with the storm
At sea and my capsized
Heart about to fall in love.

The Mystery of Vallejo

for Peter Everwine

It is said Vallejo had great favor
with the younger poets, especially after
his mysterious death. Whether he was poor
was not important, for he looked at society
with disdain.
           He came into my life
with his arrogance and brilliance –
I still remember Vallejo, the quiet,
taciturn man who could hold your
attention as he revealed the dark stars
of his experience.
           He gave his life
to poetry with little reward but
found self–satisfaction among
his fellow poets and comrades.

A Little Narrative

The day I forgot I was a poet, the heavens were clear – I
was lambasting the Mexicans; I was celebrating my birth-
day. I had my reasons for both. The posters had not
arrived announcing me as the Mexican Byron. Neither
were there any clouds proclaiming a little shade in the
afternoon. I had invited plenty of guests and girlfriends.
The topic at hand was poetry, and I felt left out of it. What
could I say that would endear me to my audience at this
point in the proceedings – before I cut the cake with no
candles, since I hate fire and the darkness beyond the fire
equally?

    I was beginning to love polemics – villanelles and
socialism had been argued both ways. I would even argue
with the devil, if he were in town. After dinner, we were
still in the mood for words. My friends got up and read
poems, the syllabics of wind. I sat there shy and quiet for
a change, since I had forgotten I was a poet. The evening
would not end soon. It lulled on into midnight on the
heat's one note. Finally, a cloud crossed the moon like one
of Byron's boats on its way to the Italian coast, and I
poured myself another quiet drink of nostalgia.

White Poplars and Mesquites
Sandia, Texas

for Luis Sr. and Ben Jr. and Josephine

Your dark eyes, Josephine, brood
like rain clouds by the white poplars
and mesquites. Tinkering twilight falling,
deer and rabbits scurrying in the meadow,
and we sit with the music of the wind,
waiting for the barbecue. . . .
                                        I quote
Shakespeare; an English professor friend
says he's a true–blooded Irishman and Indian.
I tell her I'm a Roman, and love
rabbits well cooked, though actually
I have a preference for lamb, and squab
with honey, but don't say so as we eat
savagely, and the onions taste like clouds. . . .
As the rain comes down, the evening is ripe
for love, and ends on a bloodless note.

Romancero

The little wind shares itself like a woman's
desire, and my excitement flourishes
with the greenery of the countryside.
Let desire elicit the dearest pastimes,
sing out and cajole the world from its
shark–bone misery, have a chance to dream
and follow Byron and Shelley dancing
with coteries of Italian counts, and end up
on the seashore looking for the shameless
daughters of the pagan surf. I want to
collapse on an avenue of roses, paying court
to the aristocracy and the women who
frequent my heart and sing their arias
to the wind. I want an Egyptian girl
to tell my fortune and breathe the air
of Boccaccio; I want a garland put on
my forehead so I might mingle with words
and the ladies with the astuteness of a red,
witty salamander scurrying through
the sandy river's edge as the warm sun turns
into darkness and I whirl her away from
a dream of melancholy, and the waves of the sea.

The Weather of Love

This night I saw a star
That reminded me
Of your gold earring –
Loveliness looking down
On me like floating roses
On the seashore.

If I knew you as well
As I know myself, we'd both
Be bound for hell. But love
Is love, and as incredible
As it may seem,
I've seen kisses dance
In the air like ballerinas.

Rhyme me back to my wits,
My wits as dusty
As the moon's eyes –
I feel like singing
English ballads.
I offered you a hyacinth
And a smile, the fruit
Of the season fallen
Onto the grass, touched
By the dark.
When I look to the Sierras,
Where white breasts
Touch heaven like
The nipples of madonnas,
My cloudy hands go crazy.

Poets in Exile

for the Russian poets

I sit outside in the yard
on a chair and watch
the houses, trees,
porch lights, and the
traffic that never seems
to stop.
      I'm wide awake
with the sunlight
in my arms. I ponder
the exile and executions
of the Russian poets
and the obscure bleakness
there. I watch the blue
reach of trees and wonder
how the poets must have
dreamed like I do, since
Russians are such gentle
dreamers. I go
inside, shut the door,
pick up a book,
turn its pages,
and the world groans.

III   chivalry

Into the Abyss

I go cautiously enough
Through this myopic world,
Contemptuous of half of it,
Almost content with poetry,
Seeking the verve of life,
A lover, for I need women
Like a beachcomber
Needs firewood. Christ,
There's no suspicion
On my mind that your body
And mine belong to one another
As we hurl each other
Into the abyss, but
You dress in black,
Like the dark night,
Darker than my thoughts. . . .
Then the light breaks through
As you toss your dress
Like a snakeskin
On the pillow and lie
There in the nude.
After love, your embrace
Is as soft as fog – I kiss you,
Light–headed, and fall back
Into the shadows.
After this, breakfast –
"How do you like your eggs?"

You ask. Tossed over
Lightly and over–salted.
The dishes in the washer,
You put on a halter, hug me,
And the sun delivers the day.

The Disappearance of My Wife
for Heather

I must be part magician.
Things seem to disappear on me.
I lost my handkerchief this afternoon,
And my wife, if I had one?
But to have a wife is to swim
With her, and if you lose her
In the water, there's nothing
For it.
       When I first met you,
I knew nothing – your autumn–
Colored hair and gentle eyes
Spoke a language beauty knows.
Your small breasts must have
Been persimmons, I did not see
Them. You were close for a while.
Now I'm as far away from
Your heart as the ocean in this
Late spring, with the wind
Raising its voice down the length
Of this inland valley. Still,
The flowers in the garden
Recall your radiance, and though
I just met you today, I miss you
The way I always miss the sea.

On the Front Porch

After a big meal and glasses of wine,
I'm on the front porch watching
The sunset; a woman lounging next door
With a cup of tea . . . very few shadows now,
What with the spruce and the magnolia,
Friends of the garden. In an hour
The angelic twilight will be here
On its knees, sweetening the air,
And in town, only a few streets away,
Surely the seductive ladies
With low-cut dresses of crimson or
Black, with necklaces that speak and
Sparkle like fire, will be chattering,
Just out for good times and drinks.
The men, no doubt, are out for action
As they hold their waists and buzz
Around the ladies' cheeks, the drinks
Softening their hearts like mattresses.
Soon, they will be out in the car and
Unbuttoning – she giving in like a begonia
Cut from the root, and the moon lifting
Its veil as they wrap together like
Young saplings in wind. I remember
My front porch, the road going past,
And how I got there quietly, after
Everything – and now it is midnight,
And only the sky has joined me
With its extinguished stars.

Flamenco

The wind this night of the magi
Like a woman's breast, firm, strong
Like a brooding storm,
With the green freshness of trees
And swooping birds in an orgy
Of mad freedom.
                            I write my songs
To Mexican muchachas, where
Gypsies dance and play red guitars,
Where a woman disappears from heaven
Into my arms, where we go into the abyss,
A cave of love, where the golden earth
And her body of sweet leather
Consume me like the roaring air.

Impetuous Lover

With my gift of melancholy, I give
This impetuous heart. I cannot regard
The world as simply nonsensical anymore,
But sensuous, like your fruits –
You and your lovely meadows
Of charmed flowers, picked by the muse,
Searing my lips, turning your cheeks
Into fired horizons where these fingers
Go lovingly over your cloudy twilight face
And body and see the stars, which
Praise you as I offer my gift, my basket
Of melancholies, as the sun dives
Into the sea and your aqua eyes
Burn into mine.

To a Lady I Haven't Met Yet

Your hands smooth like doves singing –
You phrase your lines with your rhyming
Aqua eyes.
                    I opened mine
And held your body of gladiolas,
Sweeping meaning ahead of us
Like an ocean wave, and you punctuating
My poems with kisses.
                    You sang
In the early moonlight as we sat down
And had a sandwich and discussed
The philosophy of dreams, of doves
Moaning on a summer day, in a puerile wind.

Senseless

There's a joy to you, gregarious like autumn,
and your gentle brown eyes that speak Spanish
and English. When I swim, you whisper
in my ear and nearly drown me as you fondle
my baroque hair and these fingers that
have forgotten to think. Your skin smooth
with beads of water, your soft lips closely
tossed by a sea storm, you dig your fingernails
into the horizon – we'll sober up, playing
with the foliage of the stars until the rhyming
sunlight. For now, don't leave me prancing
alone to talk to the leaves of the trees.
I wait for your heart to swim towards me
and knock me senseless like an ocean wave.

A Woman

She basks in the backyard
With her sunny breasts exposed,
And wants to be alone
Like some women want to be
Alone at times. The only thing is
She gets the urge for sex
And isn't comfortable
With the leaves shadowing her.
All the intelligence in the world
Won't fulfill her. So she gets up
And admires herself in the mirror,
Feels the generous fruit of her hips,
The flatness of her stomach,
And her ripe breasts.
"I'm a good woman," she says.
"A man could be happy."

Effortless

I am going to write a poem to you,
One that lulls with couplets
Your waltzing eyes and takes me
Out of despair, turning
This heart into a prickly rose
That falls and bites your neck
And arms.
              But perhaps silence
Is another word for love, and I
Should offer a silent prickly pear,
Or a rose? I've been mute before,
And now I've forgotten the rhymes
For these couplets, but with the blue
Sky persuaded by the dark, a line
Might come along and make the wind
Seem as casual as a kiss as we
Nudge each other like gentle animals.

Angry Lady

Three eggs and burnt toast
To start the day, and the finches
Outside gathering their madness,
And only bits of sunlight
Sneaking in through the heavens,
Like a lover who's seldom seen
And cruelly angry with me. . . .
Like a thrush, I become
Startled with the coming gray
Clouds; I'm a thief near twilight
When it comes to a lady
Tight with her heart.
I prepare to leave for Italy –
Buona sera to all, *buona notte*,
Signora. She prepares a road
To heaven with a cloudy face
And I surge like an ocean wave –
No more smiles or kisses
In the wrinkled clouds, only
The sky to menace me, for the sea
Was death and I was alive,
And anger has no wind
To carry me anywhere.

My Ambitions

I see you and don't see you –
The finches surround me
With glee. What a festive day
To talk to you as I look out
The window of the café. . . .

I see the plants and your green
Eyes dancing there; I remember
Giving you a chrysanthemum
From the table bouquet, and
Your smile made me want
To plant a garden.

I have a problem with my eyes
As I become a prisoner of this
Place, the ground fog crawling
In where my ambitions fly
Into my heart like the birds
Heading south for winter.

Roses

My mind is like grapes on a vine,
The cool wind like a drink of scotch,
My neighbor's music, *rancheras*,
Which bid her husband good–bye.
When he is off to work in the fields
I take her roses, tell her she has
The scent of spring on her lips.
She invites me in for tamales and coffee
And I tell her I'm an agnostic
This morning and, like the flowers,
Could not sleep. She'll pray for me
To the Virgin, she says as I put my hand
Softly on her shoulder and tell her
To pray for lovers, and call her "Chula,"
Placing kisses like petals on her cheek
And ear. I enter her mestizo body
With my melancholy and mystique,
Her brunette hair seducing
Her shoulder like shadows
From a tree, her rustic brown eyes
Dancing before me like the two
Roses I cut from her garden in the dark.

Faces the Color of Heaven

There is excitement in your eyes,
like a gazelle I've chased
and never found in a dream,
like darkness after twilight. . . .

And, dazzled by the melancholy
lines of your body, I turn
to the strong night wind
for a look at you where you quiver
like falling leaves in the darkness
as I come close to the exquisite –
as you swim deftly with me
towards shore, your deep-set eyes
singing the lyrics of a bird
straying into a window.

Storm

Your quietness
Like a dove
That fails to hum,
And your bosom
Of roses with the dark,
Crazy storm approaching.
You cuddle under
The blanket
That covers us
As we listen to
The heartbeats
Of the rain,
Its rhythm among
The green plants.
And the shoots
Of your body
Gather themselves,
And your black tresses
Flow to the blue shadows.

Loves to Drink Tea and Make Love to Women

She's so healthy – her ankles
Move to her rhythms
As her knees swivel
Like a woman in love,
And she puts me in her thoughts.
The robins are loving, and
My arms are softened by her
Embraces; her soft arms
I use to steer my boat,
And her stomach is the ocean
I fathom, deep and deeper still,
Her eyes in the sky that
Overlooks the vast sea.
I place my hands on her
Loveable plum hips,
I who love women with charm,
Courting them with my arms
And poems, who travels
With his loneliness
And drinks tea. Slowly
She puts her arms around me
Like a soft, white–dark
Womanly maguey, or a swan. . . .

Lady

You are gentle, like the lulling
Leaves in this heart that fly about
Loose like butterflies,
Like your enigmatic eyes, brown
With the beginning of autumn.
Let these lyrics give the sea dancing ardor
As the crust of the waves sounds
In our summery ears, singing
Arias with the tide as it recedes
Submissively to our kissing. . . .
And like a mariner on board,
I listen to the etude of the surf
As you study the moon,
And I watch the stars in your eyes
While you caress the wind.
Your auburn hair tosses like red
Crape myrtle blowing with the breeze,
And I sweeten you with mischief,
Like a deviltry of desire
And a bright salute.

Your Piquant Eyes

Your piquant eyes, and soft
Romantic arms – I want to dwell there,
Your lips as close as the rose petals
I bite. Your sing–song
Eyelids invite me to tease you
With a smile. A thrush on your doorstep.
Awake, the dawn is yours.
Touch it with your fingertips;
It goes through you like water.
Let me drink of it so that
I can get drunk and, in that
Drunkenness, undress your love
And go madly through the night,
Deep into the flowers of dawn.

Poem on a Woman's Ankle

Your ankle,
Incredulous and simple.
I offer kisses to the wind,
To your heart
That palpitates
Like a thrush
And sings cheerfully
Of lost winds.
I kiss your ankle,
And you gaze at me.
I return your gaze,
And your heroic ankle
Dances.

To the Girl with the Fever in Her Smile

She tosses her hair with her left
Hand, the quiet girl with the fever
In her smile. I light a cigarette
And am either a victim
Or a loathsome scoundrel?
I can't escape her sensual
Blue eyes, as lovely as the light rain
As it hits the ground between
Shadows and dying sunlight –
The effusiveness as her shy breasts
Heave in the air, and I watch
Her eyes catching me
Like a firefly at dusk.

Early Summer

after Milton

I aim a poem
Reaching its mark
To the moon.
Lavender petals fall
Over the grass –
She's as lovely
As her lovely
Green eyes that speak
Of romance
In the garden. . . .
A sensuous peach
Afternoon, which I
Drink of and become
Heroic, gentle, and
Pursue her, enamored,
Into the darkness
Of the day.

Chivalry

As the wind razzles the leaves
on the mulberry and the morning
peers into my heart, I appear
clean shaven from my house and look
outward like a mariner, listening
to the billeting surf, the blue–
eyed sky. . . .
                    If the wind
were a woman, I'd fall in love
every day, sing and call out
like the surf, the ocean's roar
crashing against the craggy rocks.
I would bring this heart closer
to you with these rustic eyes
of melancholy, waiting for the candle–
end of night to turn into a bright morning
with the sunlight of your hair and the sea,
or with the sweetness of a plum falling
at nightfall onto the summer grass.
What gifts do you desire? A rose, a cloud,
an impetuous lover chasing stars, limping . . .

IV dreaming under gray clouds

Dreaming under Gray Clouds

On this dreaming afternoon under
gray clouds about to burst,
bunched up like scoffing clergymen,
I sit on my front porch with the stillness
of a camellia. A light wind tosses
my illusions like the leaves off the magnolia,
the school kids in their autumn dress,
swaggering like pirates or Robin Hoods
who have just robbed the neighborhood
and stolen the nectar from young ladies,
remind me of my rebel youth and
of stolen hearts – my life, a gray cloud
holding onto heaven. I feel absent–
minded here and lonely without them.

I am enthused about all this, and love
has a way of warming one's ideals,
like a coat keeps away the cold. Gray clouds
clothe me, my ego jumping out of its sleeve
as I jump over the puddles of the dead,
wet leaves. I try to tolerate my illusive illusions
and go into forensics with my lines, knowing
that this life comes like the swift rain
and is gone . . . amid the storm, life's bliss
and brooding buoyancy begin.

Midsummer

A midsummer wind and the ladies
In gaudy dresses at the beaches –
I love to torment them with an eye
And plunge into the sea as a myriad
Of waves comes at me. I feel the water
And a thigh, perhaps by accident,
And let the spray acclaim me
With its salt.
              "Be famous!" they say,
"And touch the water with your hands,
Calm the sea birds in the air."
I love them, love them all above
Speech or applause. A song tumbles
With me, and the water echoes
The chorus of the girls singing
With their bodies, and I am clothed
In their sweetness, like a water snake.

Among the Autumn Flowers
and the Moon's Light

I muse over the Japanese gardens
At twilight, this green grass and
A heavenly sky, the bluebirds
Quite calm as the trees.
                              Bit by bit,
I have come to know her,
The stillness in her elusive eyes,
And I stand on the brown earth
And caress her black tresses,
Like cutting flowers in the cool
Morning. You cannot accuse me
Of being a fool, but perhaps
Of being a *romancero*, a bird
Alone amid the oaks as she sits
With her hands poised on her lap,
Her black tresses covering her
Gentle shoulders like water.
I go into the twilight, kissing
Pieces of her Oriental gardens
As if the world were ending. . . .

A Piece of Dark Cloud

With your beauty
A guy could die young
Just to be with you, . . .
And being with you
Solves problems,
With the blue–
Bird's songs
In your eyes,
And my music
The same as
The heron's hungry cry
Above the beach.
Your feet on the sand,
Your brows a
Piece of dark cloud
In the heavens –
Kisses live there.
Nevertheless,
With your beauty
A guy could die
Young just looking
At you, and the clouds
Would unfurl from within
And devastate us
With our pride

As they embrace
Darkness or melancholy
In the stormy evening,
Despite a gentle
Gypsy moon.

Moon

The bliss–sliced quarter moon,
the protagonist in hard, lawless joy –
Ariadne, with her arms of silk,
bathing in the heavens as
the muddy clouds cover her dark eyes,
and her black silver hair that falls over
her geranium breasts, which sing and sting
as he bites their shadows. . . . The moon
is covered with celestial snow, the stars
fade, and darkness follows them through
this placid night of bitten kisses
with its wick of loneliness.

Traveler in a Light Rain

after the Japanese poet Sogi

I find my words rasping in a vase
Of flowers, a song in the long afternoon.
By the hedgerow the sun caresses me
With a woman's arms and lightens
My step. The wattled Japanese
Gardens sing of the poetic traveler
Suffering with love. All I remember
Are my girlfriend's nipples
As lovely as soft almonds.
I watch her lips on my mouthy words,
Spoken softly like falling blossoms
Of the apricot, in a light misty rain
Where twilight turns me toward home.

Spring

The elms this morning looked like
They were genuflecting as I did
When I was a child,
Growing up slowly,
Like a plant stubborn in its roots.

I sit pensive with a cup of coffee,
Battling the early coolness
With a bittersweet stanza
About my senselessness. . . .
How often I have praised the sun
And ended up in and out of love –
Scorched, literally, whipped
Like a dog, and very happy about it.

Let me wait at the tail end of night
For you, dressed whiter than all
The snow in Europe. Spring does not
Tickle the arms of love, and my heart
Has no place to go as my loneliness
Stubbornly chips away at me. . . .

A Lyrical Kiss

I dreamed the moon
and how it behaved
as it turned its eyes toward
her. And I put a lyric in
her blood, by a white poplar,
on a quiet morning in winter.

I dreamed the moon,
and she was beauty
as the cold wind ran
its fingers up her spine,
a frigid kiss. I put
a lyric beside her,
in her winter blood.

Evening at the Park

I see the wild geese overhead,
Forlorn as distant clouds.
Wild–eyed, I seek her lakeside,
Feeding the ducks amid the cool
Breeze. . . . This evening,
Like the edge of dream, keeps
The beat with a rising night wind
In August. Your breath touches me
With the evening cold – but I take
Your hand, and your face brightens
Like a sunflower – and I, wild–eyed,
Find you among the flowers that rustle
In your eyes in mid August
With the mystery of tenderness.

Outside Near the Rain

I am outside near the rain –
you're not far, you've never been
far. . . . It is I who love the rain,
the next storm will not take
you from me, but will bring
us closer, like the winds
driving the white seagulls
into the waves. . . . You remain
dear, as close as the air –
I am outside near the rain. . . .

On This Energetic Day of Autumn

With the sun like a child peeking through
The sky, a chill in the romantic air,
And lovers strolling in the neighborhood,
Headed for bliss or trouble, and the wind
Sweeping away illusions and emotions
From my sidewalk, the rebels out of school,
Walking through the dying front lawn
Wearing gaudy outfits – reds, yellows,
Greens, aquas. . . . In future years
There will be others like them, treading
The same lawn, and no telling where
I'll be, or they. The birches and elms
Are shedding leaves, and the mild wind
Is like a woman who yearns for her lover,
And he is flying to Europe on her money.

And here I am, adding on the weight
Of the world and good living, accepting
Fate like a dirty coin thrown to me.
This late morning was a joy, with
The arrival of a light rain shower
As I talked to three women – I go
As a troubadour with a blue rain
Jacket, feeling handsome. It is the fervor
In their minds that I admire so much,
Not their dresses.

                  With unselfish spirit
I remain soft–spoken, I who seek knowledge
In this life. It appalls me not to be
Befriended – yet I don't know where
They will be in the future?
Should I not remove myself from evil
And sit on this chair for the rest
Of my days, writing my autobiography
And adding the devil as a character,
Turning him into a buffoon, a hunchback
Raking leaves in the wind?

V   elegy for desire

Elegy for Desire

Never borrow money
To buy flowers –
There is an exquisite aroma
To beauty, you can spot it
In the garden amid
Plenty of hyacinths.
I am Omar, the intrepid
Romancero who climbs
Balconies to ladies
Who are beautiful
And dangerously
Within reach. . . .

*   *   *

I'm merely making a statement:
I've done away with
My rancor – my mind
Is pure, the night
Darker than my thoughts. . . .

A poem is a poem,
Regardless of the color
Of her eyes
That capsize the moon's
Light across her cheeks,
That subdue the wind,
The intrigue of the sea.

*   *   *

I turn in for the night,
But your lips, your eyes,
Breasts and etc. twitch
On my tongue, and sprout
The impetuous gardenias
Of my heart. All night
I stand in the garden
And watch as you
Lay your slip by the pillow
And slowly comb your hair.

*   *   *

There's a full moon out
And I didn't even look at it –
I was carried away
By your dark eyes
As you sat there
With notes on your hands,
Musing, preparing a song,
Your lyrics glowing
With your lipstick.
And as the shadows
Darken and curl
Beyond my hands,
I turn and point
Out Venus. . . .

*   *   *

When I'm a little drunk
With desire, my brown eyes
Are aggressive as the blue
Jays on the grass.
And all day I lectured
Robins in the heat
Who told me to go
Inside where it's cool,
where I am reminded
Of a summer – your cheeks
Of peach, and lavender
Dresses on the clothesline.
I think of your lovely ears,
The crush of the sea sound
Where I smell the sweet
Air, and this elegy
Almost brightens me.

Autobiography

The Condensed Version

Out of the hospital and free from cancer, free from social
leprosy and the like, I am writing free verse again, still
whimsical and poetic with nurses, music, and ballet. . . .
There's a ham in the house, and it's me – my drama goes
back to childhood. I was an actor at age six, and Don
Quixote/Miguel Cervantes was a Spanish friend, and so
were my chums at early school. I was in love at an early
age with my cousin. My father was a merchant, yet simple
and stern. As I grew up we had our battles, but somehow
the squall reefed, and we became great friends before the
end. He made money and loved his son. What else?
I loved the sea. My mother's mother died young and was
beautiful. One of my uncles had three wives and ten
children; he was a drinker but provided and lived a full
life. I also drank until the doctors cut that out. I had a few
bad patches with the unreal. My friends helped me realize
that I'm not the only one in the world. I recall Goethe's
maxim, Don't overestimate your talent, or underestimate
that talent. And I realize that seventh heaven comes only
while I'm writing or with a good lady friend and in love.
Yet I owe my life to the devil at times, life that has treated
me tenaciously, this miscreant manic–depressive. Never-
theless, I live grandly, if a bit suspicious, and love life with
an awkward loneliness.

Aging

I've been near madness
and cruel like the sea;
don't leave me brooding
like an owl or surging
toward a crazy wave.

Tell me the world is still round
and that my heart pumps
blood and that I'm not aging
pursuing a shadow
when you throw your blouse
toward the sea and I grab it
and touch your skin, the forlorn
salt air, the surf with
a serpent's passion, where
the sun and your blue eyes
meet mid noon.
                    Let me play
these love lyrics, grab
a piece of the moon –
for I've been near madness
and cruel like the sea.

Stranger to Myself

I go about, a stranger to mornings,
Without shrubbery, needing women –
A lost spider crawling
Up her thigh, absent from rules . . .
The holy sky is theirs,
And my ambitions sting my emotions,
Unclad with desire.

Women want romance,
Men want women,
It's been said many times –
The serpent and the wind. . . .
Let's talk more –
I need to smile, and my snake-
Skin needs to be shed.

Wind

As night darkens
there is a thud in the wind.
It deadens me and the air I breathe,
my cold heart falls like an apple
from a tree.
                    I was born a disaster,
so I overcompensate.
I'm clothed by dark clouds,
and darkness follows my footsteps
like a melancholic rain.
I'm as distant as the sea
and as close as this cold wind,
the cold night that will arrest
my heart and have me looking
to the heavens and the vacant stars
for dwellings.
                    The full moon
like a clam. The sky hangs its stars,
blue evenings are decorated with jewelry,
and absence crawls the grass
as I sit alone drinking tea. I feel
fortunate, yet I'm miserable
as a dying leaf of an apricot tree
in the mist of night.
                    Oh madness,
these days and nights of careful joy,
night birds, whatever is whistling
in the eaves, sing a song for me.

Quietly

No more sadness
To greet me,
But the ocean,
With its face
Of guitars,
Its feminine heart,
And the dreamers
Going into the water.

Trees in spring
Blooming at a distance,
A sailor laughing
Under the branches –
A young woman
With the feet
Of a dove
Walking cautiously
As a nun
On her way to town.

And the dead
So quiet
That to visit them
Is like visiting
A star,
And placing
Some flowers there.

I want to thank someone,
To kiss a woman
On the seashore,
Softly, on her lips –
Like a troubadour
Going out to sea. . . .

Eurasian Girls

The patio serene, the Eurasian girls at lunch.
The wind does not die down, neither does their chatter –
The young saplings lean into each other like lovers. . . .
This is my unhappy retreat; I have to be here,
Dealing with myself and my condition – a poetic aura
On my mind, the simple loneliness of air everywhere
And words with metaphors and couplets that chase
After each other on the wind like ashes,
Like the pale violet haze of evening
Or the eyes of the Eurasian girls. . . .

This Gentle Mind at Loose Ends

Melancholy dreams have chased me
here, a sullen chill frequents
the bones of my arms.
I am the disobedient one,
the one plunging into romance
like a swimmer who comes up
half–drowned –
                           bitter or sweet,
gentle or cruel, my prepossessing
heart will sacrifice itself
ultimately to the sea.

I sit silently before a fountain,
Half–acquainted with the stars,
with the tenderness of a light rain.

To Sentiment

Oh this morning is delicious,
Recalling your body of gladiolas
And my poems punctuated
With kisses, that afternoon
We sat down with a sandwich
And discussed the philosophy
Of dreams.
                But you are away
And in my waywardness,
My late–morning melancholy,
I feel more like a bird on its
Breaking branch, trying
To balance on the air.
The kingly spruce in my yard
And the thrush with a love song –
I am sensitive to the air
And to the wind and to alluring
Mornings. I am the aging mariner
Of his youthful loneliness,
A rebel tossing pebbles
At the Pacific wind.
These chill mornings remind me
That I must remain constant
In my efforts for poetry,
For my love of the world –
Out of this life's mischief
I rebound, poet with
His heart's torn ligaments.

A Cicada Sings to Me

I am like a man at twilight – bereft,
As they used to say, of love.
A traveler worn down on the road,
Looking at the quiet shadows before me
Where I stop – so lonely, a cicada sings
To me, as the moldy evening light

Falls sighing in the fields before
The night, like me, subservient to her
Love and left in the middle of a rhyme,
Composing in the end a song, going
Lame with a lover's wound.

This Heart

No matter how sad the clouds,
I am everyone's Don Juan –
I am the hero of sunlight,
And mornings burn in your
Gold hair as the sun moors
Itself like a Spanish ship
By the bay. I would
Set sail with you, with this
Roseate heart, even as we
Separate from the darkness
Into the pillows of our fate.

Take notice of this heart –
You'll find it hard to break,
Like the buttons on a strait–
Jacket. Even as I swagger
And boast like a schoolboy,
There is no urgency. There are
Many annoyances in my life,
Yet if the horizon appears
By your side, don't be cruel
And not reveal it to me.
I have the same sinews
As yours, and this heart
Is strong, like chipped brick.

Pelicans and Waves

How morose to sit here
Amid the October plants,
Blue as the agaves
Along the cliffs,
Groping for thoughts that are
As elusive as the breeze.

I grasp at the fruit
This concluding season,
And I am the hero of my own tale
With an alchemy of sorrow
And the blemished plot.

I feel as simple as the sky –
The afternoon marches slowly
Forward like a rook,
My mind in sweet vengeance
With its aristocratic flair.

The sinister waves
Toss back and forth,
And the pelicans
Sit like preachers,
Conversing among themselves
In a language
Misunderstood for English.

I speak to someone
In the blue wind –
Her red hair flares
And falls
On my hands,
And I grab it
As she takes me
With her through
The wooded water.

Melancholy dreams have chased me
Here, a sullen chill frequents
The bones of my arms.
I am the disobedient one,
The one plunging into romance
Like a swimmer,
Half–drowned. . . .

Love of the Sea

You'll catch him there, walking backwards and forwards before the waves – realistic and unrealistic in whims and subtleties, which, like spindrift, reveal not only his loneliness and love of the sea but his chivalrous approach to the seagulls, whose antecedents go back to the romantics. And that's a long time ago, but to him, it's ever present. Passing the 20th or 21st century, pathos and sentimentality are all the same. He is turning over shells like bits of clean, clear language, piecing together love from an abstraction and a state of mind, the salt of the wind offshore.

He's learning his lines and craft. The drama has not begun, nor are the actors prepared as he begins to address the palms. Nevertheless, the ladies are here, Omar's actresses – melancholy lovers, seductive and daring, who are not only talented, beauteous charmers, but sprites turning love into a haunting song, a melody extracted from the sea.

Poem Recovering from a Stroke

This quiet day, I am
Among the fortunate few
Gathered here in the light
On the patio porch.
Yesterday, two doves
Were eaten by a mangy cat,
Vicious, like some humans.
My editor has four cats
Of his own – need I say
I prefer dogs? Regardless,
He is a good friend;
I don't feel he has anything
Against dogs, he just likes cats.

So yesterday was a cat day
As I recalled the crush
Of the sea, a terrible
Crashing melody. Still,
I'm here trying to persuade
The world of my talent,
With no forgiveness or excuses.
The heavens change color,
And I can think of soldiers
Who are slaughtered
Without any warning.
The fact is, there can be
Vicious dogs as well.

This is not a safe world.
Only for a fortunate few,
And even then, disasters
Strike like a snake, and
The blossoms of early summer
Burst, dropping their petals. . . .

Sometimes

Sometimes, and near sometimes, I feel aging, but then again my second youth and romanticism flash through my veins like a silver fish and I'm young again. The girls I've loved, those I haven't, and the women I might love, all make up for my sadness and intoxicating illusions. I have no fear of ending up unknown or unrecognized. The time I dedicate to my work is the time I dedicate to life, its many roads, and all its random beauty. If somebody tells me I'm old, I answer, "Old for what?" Tell me what you know, and I'll tell you something you don't. Poetry is not ideas. If I lean on my cane too heavily, it's because I won't sit down for anything; I'm a born fighter, a lover of the solid earth.

Acknowledgments

Thanks to the editors of the following publications where some of these poems first appeared:

Artful Dodge, "Love of the Sea"

The Bloomsbury Review, "Here and Now"

Hotel Amerika, "A Little Narrative"

HUBBUB, "Effortless"

The Journal, "This Heart"

LUNA, "Ode to the Night Air," "Quietly," "To a Lady I Haven't Met Yet," "Impetuous Lover," "Flamenco," "A Cicada Sings to Me"

The Montserrat Review, "Faces the Color of Heaven"

Poetry International, "Roses," "My Melancholy," "My Ambitions," "My Gentle Dog," "Angry Lady," "On This Energetic Day of Autumn"

Runes, A Review of Poetry, "A Piece of Dark Cloud"

Snake Nation Review, "Pelicans and Waves," "Elegy for Desire," "Men at Sea," "Autobiography: The Condensed Version"

Special thanks as always to Jon Veinberg and Christopher Buckley for editing help and support.

About the Author

Luis Omar Salinas has been a leading Chicano poet since the publication of his first book, *Crazy Gypsy*, in 1970. Born in Robstown, Texas, he has spent most of his life in California, especially in the small towns in or around Fresno. Early in his writing career, he worked with Henri Coulette, Philip Levine, Peter Everwine, and Robert Mezey. Salinas has authored seven collections of poetry and many chapbooks. His books have long been classics of Chicano literature and include *Afternoon of the Unreal* (1980), *Prelude To Darkness* (1981), *Darkness Under the Trees / Walking Behind the Spanish* (1982), and *The Sadness of Days: Selected and New Poems* (1987). In 1997, his last book, *Sometimes Mysteriously*, won Salmon Run Press's National Book Contest. With Lillian Faderman, Salinas co-edited *From The Barrio: A Chicano Anthology* (1973), and over the last thirty-five years his poems have been widely anthologized.

Recognized for his original and significant contribution to contemporary letters, Salinas has received the Early Lyon Award, the Stanley Kunitz Award, and a General Electric Foundation Award. In 1985 he read at the Library of Congress with Sandra Cisneros.

A pioneer in Chicano/Latino literature, Salinas is one of its most senior poets and a prominent voice in contemporary American poetry. He lives and writes in Sanger, California.